• LEARNING HOW •

Football

BY
SUE BOULAIS

Bancroft-Sage Publishing

601 Elkcam Circle, Suite C-7, P.O. 355 Marco, Florida 33969-0355 USA

• LEARNING HOW •
Football

AUTHOR
SUE BOULAIS

EDITED BY
JODY JAMES

DESIGNED BY
CONCEPT and DESIGN

I would like to dedicate this book to the quartet of faithful football fans in my family: Mom, Dad, Mike, and Chuck.

PHOTO CREDITS
All Sport: Mike Powell - Page 4, 5, 12, 15, 21;
Scott Halleran - Pages 17, 19, 45;
Bettmann Archive: Page 7.
Gallery Nineteen: Gregg Anderson - Pages 8, 10, 18, 27, 33b, 34, 36, 38, 39, 41, 43;
Brent Johnson - Pages 11, 23, 25b, 42.
Jim Kirk: Page 30.
Mitchell B. Reibel: Cover, Pages 9, 16, 20, 25a, 31, 33a, 35, 37.
Diagrams By: Concept and Design - Pages 14, 29.

ACKNOWLEDGMENTS
I would like to thank Mr. Frank Moletteire, president of Boys and Girls Clubs of Central Florida, and staff members Joe Moletteire, George Sigler and Larry Dorsey for their help and technical expertise. They provided assistance and details concerning youth league football that I was unable to obtain anywhere else. Thanks also to David Nelson, Jim Mehrman, MAYAA, and the Mankato Loyola and Cleveland High School football teams for their help.

TABLE OF CONTENTS

**LIBRARY OF CONGRESS
CATALOGING-IN-PUBLICATION DATA**

Boulais, Sue.
   Learning how: football / by Sue Boulais; edited by Jody James; illustrated by Concept and Design.
       p.   cm. – (Learning how sports)
   Summary: Describes the equipment, rules, techniques, and safety aspects of football.
   ISBN 0-944280-37-4 (lib. bdg.) – ISBN 0-944280-43-9 (pbk.)
   1. Football – Juvenile literature. [1. Football.]   I. Title.   II. Series

796.332–dc20   91-24876
                                                                                CIP
                                                                                AC

**International Standard
Book Number:**
Library Binding 0-944280-37-4
Paperback Binding 0-944280-43-9

**Library of Congress
Catalog Card Number:**
91-24876

INTRODUCTION

The teams face each other, crouched along the line of scrimmage. The quarterback calls the signals. The center snaps him the ball. Immediately, the linemen block the oncoming team. They must protect the quarterback. The quarterback drops back and throws the ball to a receiver down the field. Catching the ball, the receiver charges toward the end zone. He dodges most of the players trying to stop him. But they tackle him ten yards from the goal line. The players line up for another play.

Today's football games are well organized, carefully planned, and skillfully played. Every player trains and practices special moves. Every player knows and follows the same strict rules on the field. Every player wears special gear to make the rough, often dangerous game as safe as possible.

The quarterback calls the signals to begin a play.

The receiver charges toward the end zone.

English colonists brought "futballe" with them when they came to the New World. The English had been playing this kick-the-ball game since the 1100s. A large team of boys from one town would try to kick a "ball" down the main street of the other team's town. The "ball" was a cow's bladder filled with air.

"Futballe" didn't change much for more than 200 years. Then, in 1823, a player got angry and disgusted during a game at England's Rugby School. Instead of kicking the ball, he picked it up and started to run with it. The other players were surprised, but they quickly stopped the runner by tackling him (pushing him to the ground and falling on him). The game with its new moves—running with the ball and tackling—was named *rugby football*, after the school. "Futballe"—in which players only kicked the ball—became known as *soccer*.

The new rugby moves quickly reached America. Later, in the 1880s, American football began to change even more. Over the next forty years, slowly but surely, the game became more and more like the football you watch today.

By the 1920s, American college football had firm rules. Players could use five basic moves during a game: kicking, running, tackling, blocking, and passing. More and more colleges formed teams. High schools began to put together teams, too.

Professional football was also becoming more popular. In 1920, the American Professional Football Association was formed. Two years later, the Association changed its name to the National Football League (NFL). Today, the NFL is still America's chief professional football league.

By the 1920s, American college football had firm rules and the American Professional Football Association was formed. This photo was taken in 1936.

CHAPTER ONE:

Football Equipment

Football players use special equipment that is very different from equipment for other ball games. Football uniforms are much more complex than uniforms for most other sports. Even the football itself is different from other types of balls.

The Football

Of all the balls used in American sports, only a football is not round. It is about 11 inches long and 7 inches in diameter at the center. It is made of four pieces of leather sewn together. Leather laces along one seam provide a grip so that players can catch, hold, and pass the ball.

A football has a rubber lining that is filled with air. An inflated football weighs about 14 to 15 ounces.

A football is made of four pieces of leather sewn together.

Football Uniform

Football is a *contact* sport. Players hit each other and knock each other down. Their uniforms help keep the players from getting seriously hurt. No player goes out on the field until properly "suited up."

Good football equipment is absolutely necessary for safe playing. Even if you are a beginner, you need to wear good equipment. You might be able to use equipment that older players or brothers have outgrown. But make sure that used equipment is still in good shape and fits properly. Wearing equipment that doesn't fit correctly can be more dangerous than wearing no equipment at all.

Football is a contact sport. Good football equipment is necessary for safe playing.

Helmet

A football helmet is your most important piece of equipment. It protects your skull from head blows that could cause serious injury. Your helmet should fit on your head comfortably and firmly. The back should cover your skull, and the frontpiece should be about 1 or 1 1/2 inches above your eyebrows.

Helmets also have a chin strap and a face mask. The chin strap keeps the helmet from being easily knocked off. The face mask helps protect your eyes, nose, and mouth from injury. The kind of face mask you need depends on the position you play.

The helmet is your most important piece of equipment.

Mouthpiece

The mouthpiece protects your teeth and helps prevent concussions and broken jaws. Mouthpieces come in different styles. You can attach some kinds of mouthpieces to your face mask. After you buy your mouthpiece, be sure to have your dentist fit it to your mouth. A perfect fit is important, especially if you wear braces.

Shoulder pads

Your shoulder pads should cover your whole shoulder area. The under pad should extend just beyond the tip of your shoulders. You should be able to move your arms freely. Your shoulders will be measured from tip to tip to get your proper size.

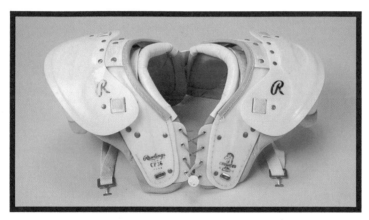

Shoulder pads should cover your whole shoulder area.

Rib or kidney pads

When you block or get tackled, your kidneys can get hurt very easily. Rib or kidney pads help protect your kidneys and other vital organs. To get the right fit, your chest will be measured as if you were buying a suit jacket.

Hip pads

You can wear one of two different kinds of hip pads. Some are made as part of football pants. Another kind of hip pad comes separately on a belt.

Thigh and knee pads

These pads fit into pockets inside your football pants. They should be just big enough to cover the area they protect. If the pads are too big, or if they move around when you play, they can keep you from moving freely and may cause you to get hurt. If you have the right-sized pants and pads, the pads will feel snug against your legs, and they will protect your thighs and knees well.

Thigh and knee pads should fit snugly against your legs.

12

Supporter

All male players should always wear an athletic supporter while playing football. Some leagues require that the supporter contain a protective cup as well.

Pants and jersey

Both jersey and pants should fit tightly over your protective equipment, covering it and keeping it in place. Neither your jersey nor your pants should be so tight that you can't move freely, however.

Shoes

Football shoes are sturdy and usually made of leather. The soles have **cleats** that give you a firm footing, whether you play on grass or **artificial turf**. Many players also tape their ankles before a game to provide further support.

CHAPTER TWO:

The Football Field

A standard high school, college, or professional football field is a level rectangle 53 1/3 yards wide and 120 yards long. Youth league fields can vary in length according to a league's requirements. The field's surface can be real grass or artificial turf at all levels of play.

Each long side of the field is marked by a *sideline*. Players who touch or cross a sideline are ruled out of bounds. Inside the sidelines, two rows of dashed lines run the length of the field. These are the *hash marks*. Every football play starts with the ball between or on the hash marks.

White *yardage lines* run across the field from sideline to sideline. Yardage lines show where the ball is placed and how far a team has to go for a first down and score. There is a yardage line every five yards. The lines are numbered every ten yards. The 50-yard line is at the middle of the field. Each goal line is 50 yards from mid-field. An end zone extends ten yards past each goal line.

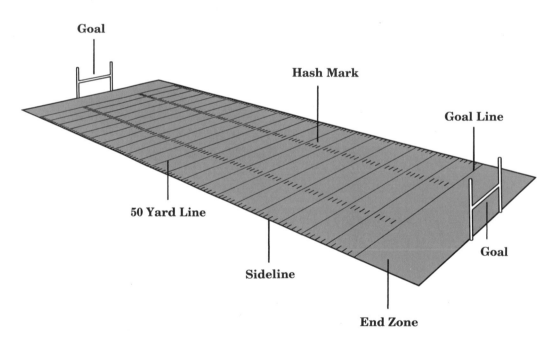

CHAPTER THREE:

The Teams: Players and Positions

The most important word in football is *teamwork*. Eleven players from each team are on the field during the game. The players on each team must work together if they want to score and win the game.

The team with the ball is the offensive team, or the *offense*. Their job is to get the football down the field and across the other team's goal line for a **touchdown**. The offensive players try to score by running with the ball. They can also pass, or throw, the ball to another player on their team who may be nearer the goal. That player then tries to get the ball over the goal line.

The offensive players try to score by running with the ball.

The team without the ball is the defensive team, or the *defense*. Their job, of course, is to stop the offense from making touchdowns. The defensive team members try to tackle the player with the ball. They also try to make an **interception** when offensive players pass the ball.

Each college and professional football team has offensive, defensive, and special *squads*, or units. All three squads play different parts in a football game. When a team has the ball, its offensive squad is on the field. When the team loses the ball, its offensive squad leaves the field, and its defensive squad goes into action. The team's special squad does its job at the game's kickoff and after each touchdown, whenever a field goal is attempted for a score, and in punting situations.

Each squad has its own set of coaches. The coaches help the players learn and work on the plays and skills they need. The coaches also help the squads learn to work together as a team.

The defensive team tries to tackle the player with the ball.

The Offensive Team

The players on an offensive team include the linemen, the quarterback, and the running backs. The offensive team usually lines up for play in a **T-formation**. The T-formation is one of the oldest and most basic offense arrangements. Seven linemen must always make up the line of the T-formation. On any play, the offensive linemen line up along the **line of scrimmage**. This imaginary line marks where the ball ended up on the last play.

The line of scrimmage marks where the ball ended up on the last play.

The linemen are the center, two guards, two tackles, and two ends. The center plays in the middle of the line, and has two jobs. The first is to **snap**, or give, the football to the quarterback. The center's snap begins every play. The center's second job is **blocking**. As soon as the ball is snapped, the center must block a player on the defensive team.

On either side of the center are the guards. Next to each guard is a tackle. Guards and tackles block defensive players who are trying to stop the offense's ball carrier.

The ends are the players at either end of the line. Like the center, the ends have two jobs. They block defensive players. However, ends are also **eligible receivers**. That means that they can receive, or catch, a ball thrown by the quarterback.

The quarterback is behind the linemen. He is squarely in back of, and very close to, the center. The quarterback is the "boss" of the offensive team. He tells the other players what moves, or plays, to make. He calls the **signals** to start each play. He must make quick, intelligent decisions.

The center snaps the football to the quarterback. This snap begins every play.

After the center snaps the ball, the quarterback has three choices. He can **hand off** the ball to a running back. He can run down the field carrying the ball himself. Finally, he can drop back and pass the ball to an end or a running back.

Directly behind the quarterback is a fullback. On either side of the fullback crouch the halfbacks. These players are also called *running backs*. They block for the quarterback if the quarterback decides to run the ball. But, like the ends, running backs are eligible receivers. They can receive the football from the quarterback and run with it.

The quarterback can hand off the ball to a running back, carry the ball himself, or pass it to an end or running back.

The Defensive Team

The players on a defensive team include defensive linemen, linebackers, and defensive backs. The number of each kind of player depends on the kind of game the offense is playing. In any case, there can only be eleven defensive players on the field at one time.

Defensive linemen line up directly across from the offensive linemen. There can be from three to seven linemen, depending on the play. The noseguard, or middle guard, is the defensive lineman who lines up directly across from the center. The guard's job is to stop any plays that the offense tries to run up the middle of the line.

On either side of the noseguard are the tackles. The tackles also stop running plays. In addition, they try to **sack** (tackle behind the line of scrimmage) the quarterback if he

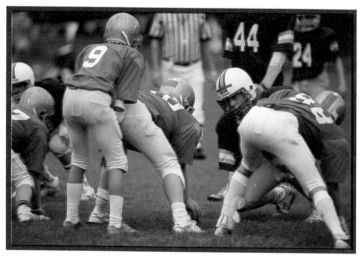

Defensive linemen line up directly across from the offensive linemen.

tries to pass the ball. Even if they don't succeed in sacking the quarterback, their attempt rushes, or hurries, the quarterback as he tries to throw the ball.

On the outside of the tackles are the ends. They stop players that try to go around them. They can also help the tackles sack the quarterback.

Right behind the defensive linemen are the linebackers. Three or four linebackers may be on the field, depending on the play. These players try to stop running plays that come toward their area.

Behind the linebackers are the defensive backs. Their job is different from that of the rest of the defensive team. The defensive linemen and linebackers try to stop running plays. The defensive backs try to stop passes.

There are two types of backs: cornerbacks and safeties. Cornerbacks cover the area between the line of scrimmage and the sidelines. Safeties are **roving players**. They can go anywhere in the field area. Their job is to cover center field and intercept the football when the quarterback passes it.

Players on the defensive team will try to sack or rush the quarterback.

Special Teams

College and professional football teams have squads called *special teams*. Each player on the special teams squad does just one job. These players may be called into the game at any time to do their jobs. When a special teams player comes out on the field, a player from his team must leave the field. There can be no more than eleven team members on the field at one time.

The place-kicker is the special teams player who makes the opening **kickoff**. The kickoff starts a football game. A place-kicker also kicks the football when the team is trying for a field goal. The kicker may use a *kicking tee* or another team member called a holder to hold the ball in the kicking position.

Another player in the place-kicking unit is the center. The center gets any kick started with a **long snap**. For a long snap, the center stands 10-15 yards in front of the punter or 7 yards from the holder for the place-kicker.

A punter is another kind of kicker. The punter drops the football and kicks it as it falls. The punter usually kicks the ball when his team hasn't made a first down (gained ten yards) in three plays. If the offense decides to give the ball to the other team on the fourth play, the punter is called in to kick the ball as deep into the other team's area as possible.

A kick returner is a player who catches the ball after the kickoff and starts it back down the field. During a kickoff, two kick returners are usually placed on the field, one on each side. One kick returner goes onto the field to return a punt. They complete the play, either by being tackled or by calling for a **fair catch**. Then they hand the ball over to their team's offensive unit, and regular play begins.

The kick returner signals for a fair catch.

CHAPTER FOUR:

Playing a Football Game

Passing, running, blocking, tackling, kicking: players can combine these five plays in hundreds of ways. No matter how they combine the plays, each team has the same purpose: to score while keeping the other team from scoring.

Teams can score in four ways. The most exciting way is to make six points with a touchdown. A touchdown is scored when a player runs the ball over the other team's goal line. A player can also catch a pass in the end zone for a touchdown.

After scoring a touchdown, a team always tries for a **conversion**. This is a chance to make one more point by kicking the ball over the crossbar and between the uprights of the goalposts. A conversion is often called "the extra point."

A team can score three points by making a **field goal**. To make a field goal, the place-kicker kicks the ball over the crossbar and between the uprights on the opponent's goalposts.

The defensive team can score two points by trapping a ball carrier in his own end zone. This score is called a **safety**.

Running for a touchdown is an exciting way to score points.

This kicker and holder are practicing for a field goal. The ball must be kicked over the crossbar and between the uprights on the opponent's goalposts.

The teams have 60 minutes of playing time in which to score. That time period is divided into two halves of 30 minutes each. The halves are divided into two quarters of 15 minutes each, with a minute of rest time between each quarter. Between halves is a 20-minute rest break called **half-time.**

A football game usually takes about three hours. The game takes this long because **officials** stop the clock at several points during the game. The clock stops after a team scores, after an incomplete pass, after an out-of-bounds play, and when a penalty is called. Each team can also call three time-outs during each half.

Before the game begins, the officials and team captains meet on the 50-yard line for a coin toss. The toss determines who receives the ball and which goal each team defends. At the beginning of the third quarter, the decisions are reversed.

All football games begin with a kickoff. The special teams squad lines up along their own 35-yard line. Facing them ten yards away is the *receiving* team. The kick returner stands far down the field, waiting to catch the ball.

When the referee blows a whistle, the kicker and the offensive team start moving. The kicker sends the ball soaring far down the field. A kick returner catches it and heads back down the field. The other defensive players try to block as many opposing players as they can. They want the returner to get the ball as far back up the field as possible.

When the kick returner is finally tackled, officials mark the place where the returner was brought down. This becomes the line of scrimmage for beginning regular play. The special team players leave the field. The offensive and defensive teams come out.

The first thing both teams do is **huddle**. The offense makes a circle around the quarterback. The quarterback tells the team what the play will be. He also tells the team what number or color will signal the center to snap the ball. The huddle breaks, and the offense comes to the line of scrimmage. They line up in formation, ready and alert.

In the defensive huddle, the players think of all the possible plays the offense might try. They decide on plays that they think will stop the offense. The defensive huddle breaks, and the players line up across the line of scrimmage from the offense.

The offensive team tries to move the ball by running or passing. The defensive team tries to stop the offense by tackling the runner. The defense can also try to intercept the ball. If the defense intercepts, their team gets control of the ball and their offensive unit comes onto the field.

The team huddle is where the players agree on their next play or on how to stop their opponents.

The offense has four tries, or **downs**, to advance the ball ten yards closer to the opposing team's goal line. If the offense moves the ball ten yards, the team earns a first down. A first down allows the offense another four downs to make another ten yards.

No matter how hard or how well the offensive team is working, the defensive team is working just as hard. By tackling and intercepting, they make it as difficult as possible for the offense to move the ball.

Both offense and defense use many different plays during a game. How do they know which ones to use?

Every football team has a **playbook**. The playbook describes in detail each and every play a team can use. These plays are put together by the coaches and players.

Each team also watches films of the other team playing football. Each team formulates a **game plan** of plays that they think will beat the other team's plays.

As the teams battle up and down the field, the officials keep a sharp eye out. The chief official of each crew is the *referee*. The officials' job is to make sure the game runs smoothly and safely. Officials are the ones who call **penalties** for rule infractions and **fouls**.

A player who breaks a playing procedure rule commits a rule infraction. **Offsides** is an example of a rule infraction. Officials call an offsides against a player who crosses the line of scrimmage before the center snaps the ball to the quarterback. The penalty for a rule infraction is usually five yards. (This means that the team whose player broke the rule must move back five yards closer to their own goal line.)

Fouls are more serious. Officials declare a foul when players break the rules that are meant to protect them from getting hurt. Officials call fouls when a player uses more physical force than he should to stop a play (unnecessary roughness) or displays unsportsmanlike conduct. Fouls usually cost a team 15 yards. Sometimes the officials even order a player off the field if he deliberately begins a fight or uses unnecessary roughness.

Officials also keep track of the game's official time and stop the clock for time outs. They signal when a play has ended. They also rule on scores.

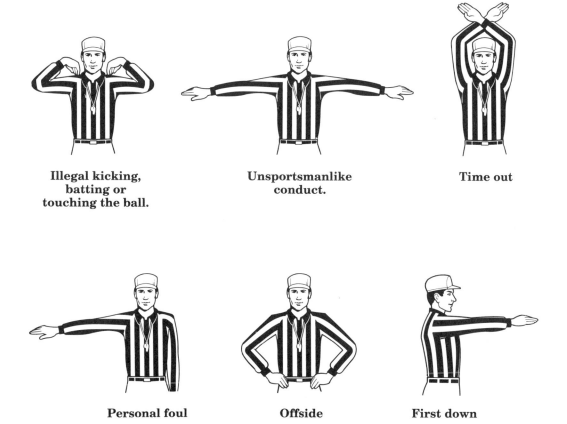

Illegal kicking, batting or touching the ball.

Unsportsmanlike conduct.

Time out

Personal foul

Offside

First down

CHAPTER FIVE:

Learning Football Skills

Now you can try football's five basic moves: passing, running, blocking, tackling, and kicking. Remember— football is a *team* sport. You will need a friend to practice with you.

Do not forget to wear your protective gear. Wearing your helmet and pads is very important. Football is a contact game. You will hit other players and knock them down, and they will do the same to you. Your helmet and padding will help keep you from being seriously hurt.

Ready? Go! Read each of the next sections carefully and study the pictures. You will soon be on your way.

Football is a team sport.

The game begins with teamwork and planning plays together.

Football is a contact game, so good protective gear is very important.

Centering the Ball

Centers learn two ways to handle the football: a *T-formation snap* and a *long snap*. In the T-formation snap, a center hands the ball back through his legs to the quarterback. Pros snap the ball with one hand, but while you're learning, use both hands.

Place your feet at least a shoulder-width apart and parallel to each other. Bend over and place your hands on the ball. Keep your thumbs on the seams and point your other fingers down. Point the front of the football up at a 45-degree angle.

When you snap the ball, the laces should go toward the quarterback's throwing hand. If your quarterback is right-handed, turn the football's laces *down*. If your quarterback is left-handed, turn the laces *up*.

The quarterback stands directly behind you. His hands are under you, so close to your seat that you can feel them. As you snap the ball, the quarterback's hands move forward to meet it. As soon as you have snapped the ball, you begin to block the defensive player right in your path.

A center must also learn how to make a *long snap*. A long snap can go to the punter or to the holder for a place-kicker.

Spread your feet wider than usual. Stretch both arms fully in front of you. Have your throwing hand under the ball, and grip it as if you were going to throw a forward pass. Steady the ball by putting your other hand on top of the ball. When the punter calls the snap signal, swing the ball back and let go of it as it passes between your legs. Follow through with your arms and rotate your hands to make the ball spiral. Look back between your legs to spot your target: the punter's waist.

This photo shows the center doing a T-formation snap.

This photo shows the center attemping a long snap.

Passing the Ball

Remember that a forward pass is one way to advance the ball. Knowing how to pass is an important, necessary skill.

Grip the ball in your throwing hand. Form a "U" at the pointed end of the football with your thumb and fingers. Your fingers should go over the ball's laces. The ball should feel comfortable and balanced in your hand.

Hold the ball at ear level. Sweep your arm back and forth a couple of times. (Don't let the ball go.) If you can do this and control the ball, you have a good grip.

The following instructions explain how to throw a forward pass right-handed. If you are left-handed, just

The ball should feel comfortable and balanced in your hand when passing.

substitute "left" for "right," and "right" for "left." Hold the ball in front of your body, as if the center had just thrown it to you. Drop back several steps and bring the ball up to shoulder level. Make sure your right foot is in back, and put all your weight on it.

Extend the ball back behind your right shoulder. Quickly turn your hand so that the ball's tip is in direct line with your target (your receiver). Shift your weight forward to your left foot and whip your throwing arm forward with an overhand motion.

As the ball starts to roll off your fingertips, whip your wrist down. The downward move of your wrist will make the football spiral through the air instead of wobbling. Be sure to finish your move by **following through** with your arm.

When making a forward pass, be sure to finish your move by following through with your arm.

Receiving and Running

The most accurate pass in the world isn't any good if the receiver doesn't catch the ball. Receiving and running are skills that all players need. Remember, any defensive player can intercept the ball!

The most important rule in receiving is *keep your eye on the ball.* Don't think about anything else for the moment. Pretend that ball flying toward you is the only thing in the world as you run toward it. When you are within a few strides of the ball, reach up and grab it with your fingers.

If you are receiving a long pass as you run toward the goal line, you may have to catch the ball over your shoulder. This is difficult to do. You must run with your

You must keep your eyes on the ball when receiving a pass.

hands up in front of you while you look over your shoulder. You will need a lot of practice to be able to catch the ball this way.

Once you've caught the ball, tuck it close to your body. Now the most important thing is to protect the ball so you don't **fumble**, or drop, it. A fumble can be recovered by the opposing team.

Hold the ball with both hands like a cradle if you see a lot of linemen ready to hit you from all sides. If you are carrying the ball across an open field, hold the ball in the arm *away* from the tacklers and closest to the sidelines.

After receiving a pass, hold the ball in the arm away from the tacklers and closest to the sidelines.

Blocking

Without good blocking, the best plays can not work. Blockers clear the way for a runner and protect a passer.

Whether you are practicing a block for a runner or for a passer, you start with the *stance*. There are two versions of this position: the three-point and the four-point stance.

Three-point stance

Place your feet about a shoulder-width apart. The heel of your left foot should be in line with the toe of your right foot.

Squat and lean forward. Put the knuckles and thumb of your right hand to the ground and lean forward so that your hand takes some weight. Be sure that your shoulders and hips are even, and that your weight is on the balls of your feet. Place your left forearm on the inside of your left thigh.

The three-point stance.

Four-point stance

This stance is just like the three-point stance except that you place both hands on the ground. Practice both stances until you can do them automatically.

Once you've learned your stances, you can start practicing blocks. At first, you may want to work with a dummy.

The four-point stance.

The best way to start practicing blocks is with a dummy.

Blocking for a running play

To block for a running play, most offensive linemen use a shoulder block. As the center snaps the ball to the quarterback, come off your stance in a low charging position. Keep your head up, and aim for the middle, hip, or shoulder of the defensive lineman across from you. Hit the player with your shoulder. *Never use your head.*

When you hit your opponent, dig your feet into the ground. Try to drive the player back with short, choppy steps. Make sure, too, that you are pushing in the direction *opposite* the way the runner is headed.

Blocking for a pass

For a pass play, offensive linemen must give the quarterback both room and time to throw. Begin in a three-point stance, but put less weight on your hand. On the snap, quickly step to the inside and stand up. As you are rising, bring your arms toward your chest. Raise your elbows and put your fists together.

Hit the defensive lineman once with your shoulders, forearms, and fists. (Don't extend your arms, open your fists, or grab the lineman's jersey. If you do, you will be guilty of offensive holding.) Step back for a split second, then step forward again to meet the lineman with another good hit. Keep doing this until the quarterback throws the ball. If you can give the quarterback five seconds, you have done your job well.

Tackling

A missed tackle can mean a touchdown for the other team, so practice your tackling as well as your blocking. As with blocking, you may want to practice with a dummy first.

Your "ready" position before you tackle your opponent is called *breakdown*. Put your legs a shoulder-width apart and your weight evenly on both feet. Bend your knees and put your arms out in front of you.

Find the ball carrier quickly. Head for the same spot as the carrier. Keep your head up and your eyes on the carrier's belt buckle or middle. When you are ready to make contact, hit the carrier's midsection with your shoulders, *never* with your head. Wrap your arms around the upper legs. Drive with your legs to bring the ball carrier down.

The breakdown position, before tackling an opponent.

When making a tackle, hit the ball carrier's midsection with your shoulders and wrap your arms around the upper legs.

Kicking

A kicker is the "player with the golden foot." It takes long hours of practice to make the football go a long way in the right direction. Because of a football's odd shape, learning to kick it well may take you more than a little while.

Place-kicking

A place-kick is a toe kick. When you practice, put the ball on a kicking block or tee. Stand three steps behind the ball, with your feet about a shoulder-width apart. To kick with your right foot, line your right toe up with the ball holder. Take a step with your right foot, then a faster step with your left. Swing your right leg forward with the knee slightly bent. As you kick the ball, straighten your leg out. To kick with your left leg, reverse the "lefts" and "rights" in the instructions above.

Try to kick the ball near the bottom so it will travel high and be harder to block. Keep your head down and your

Approach to the place-kick.

Follow through after the kick.

eyes on the spot *where the ball was* as you follow through with your leg.

Punting

Punting is an instep kick. You kick the ball with the shoelace part of your shoe. Tie your shoelaces to the back or sides of your shoes. Then they will be out of the way when you kick.

Hold the ball with the laces up. Put your left hand on top of the ball near the front. Put your right hand on the side of the ball with your fingers wrapped underneath. Holding the ball this way will help you control it better.

Take a step forward with your non-kicking leg, holding the ball straight out in front of you. As you step forward with your kicking leg, drop the ball onto your foot. Your foot is already swinging up to meet the ball. After you make the kick, follow through with your kicking leg until it is over your head. As you did with the place-kick, keep your eyes on the ball at all times.

When attempting a punt, hold the ball with the laces up. Put your left hand on top of the ball near the front.

CHAPTER SIX:

Getting—and Staying—in Shape

To learn your skills and to play football, you must be healthy and in good shape. Being in shape is something you must work at all year.

There are some things you can do to stay in shape. The following instructions will help you get started. However, be sure to check with your doctor or gym teacher before you start any exercise program.

1. Exercise every day. Jumping jacks, windmills, overhead stretches, sidebends, hamstring stretches, bent-knee sit-ups, push-ups, and high knee rolls are some exercises you should do daily. Always do some "warm-up" exercises before you practice or play football. Have your gym teacher show you the proper way to do each exercise.

2. Run every day. Running helps build your speed and endurance. You will be able to play longer and better if you run every day. Again, ask your doctor how long and how far you should run.

3. Eat and drink properly. Eat three good meals a day. Try not to snack in between. Drink eight glasses of water every day, or even more if you exercise or play a great deal.

4. Get enough sleep. You need between eight and ten hours of sleep every night.

5. Do not smoke, drink, or use drugs. All three harm your body and keep your mind from working at its best.

CONCLUSION

Football is a game of skill, strength, and teamwork. Football is also a game filled with fun. Whether you join a youth league, or toss a football around the backyard with your family, you'll be playing—and enjoying—one of America's favorite sports.

Football is a game filled with fun.

GLOSSARY

artificial turf - a nonliving covering on the football field that is not natural grass; used on indoor football fields

blocking - clearing the way for a runner or passer

cleats - round, raised pieces of rubber on the soles of football shoes that help players get a better footing on the field

conversion - the single point that a team can earn after a touchdown by kicking the ball between the uprights and over the crossbar of the goalposts

down - a single play by the team that has possession of the ball

eligible receivers - the players on the offensive team who can legally catch a pass from the quarterback, including ends and running backs

fair catch - a signal by the kick returner that he does not want to run with the ball or be tackled; the line of scrimmage is then located at the place on the field where the kick returner signaled the fair catch

field goal - the three points earned by a team who kicks the ball over the crossbar and between the uprights (except after a touchdown)

following through - extending the motion of the arm or leg after passing or kicking the ball

foul - a violation of rules that are meant to keep players from getting hurt

fumble - losing control of the ball while trying to pass, catch, or run with it

game plan - the overall series of offensive and defensive plays that teams plan to use during a game

half-time - a 20-minute rest period between the second and third quarters of a football game

hand off - a play in which the quarterback gives or tosses the football to a running back after the center snaps the ball

huddles - circles formed by offensive and defensive players before each play; allows the quarterback or defensive captain to give the team instructions about the play coming up

interception - the play in which a defensive player catches a forward pass thrown by an offensive player

kickoff - the means of putting the ball in play at the beginning of the game, at halftime, and after each touchdown

line of scrimmage - the imaginary line along which players line up for each play

long snap - a snap to a punter or holder; sets the ball in position to be kicked

neutral zone - the few inches of space between the offensive and defensive lines before a snap

officials - people who enforce the rules of the game

offside - a rule infraction in which a player moves at the line of scrimmage before the center snaps the ball

penalty - the number of yards a team has to move back toward its own goal line as a result of a rule infraction or foul

playbook - a book that contains team plays and other instructions

roving player - usually the defensive safety; this player is not assigned to guard a player or a special part of the field; he can go, or rove, anywhere on the field to stop the offense

sack - tackling the quarterback behind the line of scrimmage before he can make a pass

safety - a score of two points awarded a team who traps a ball carrier in his own end zone

signal - the special word that tells the center to snap the ball to the quarterback; agreed upon in the huddle before a play

snap - the action of handing or throwing the ball to the quarterback; performed by the center

T-formation - offensive formation in which the three backs are behind the quarterback and center in a line to make a "T"

touchdown - a score of six points awarded a team who runs or passes the ball across the opposing team's goal line

Dear Readers,

You can play football at almost any age. Football leagues and clubs have divisions for players from age seven all the way to adult. The players are usually divided by age, weight, and skill level, too.

Football rules and requirements are *modified* from level to level. That means that some rules and requirements are different at each level. For example, the football field for younger players is not so long as the football field for college or professional players.

If you join a football league, remember that your coach is the boss. Listen to, learn, and follow the directions that your coach gives you.

Be sure to check with your doctor, too, before you join a youth football league. Football is a "rough-and-tumble" sport. Your doctor will help you decide whether it's the right sport for you.

The Author, Sue Boulais